Oxford University Press, Great Clarendon Street, Oxford OX2 6DP

Oxford   New York
Athens   Auckland   Bangkok   Bogota   Bombay
Buenos Aires   Calcutta   Cape Town   Dar es Salaam   Delhi
Florence   Hong Kong   Istanbul   Karachi
Kuala Lumpur   Madras   Madrid   Melbourne
Mexico City   Nairobi   Paris   Singapore
Taipei   Tokyo   Toronto

and associated companies in
Berlin   Ibadan

OXFORD and OXFORD ENGLISH
are trade marks of Oxford University Press

ISBN International edition 0 19 435108 4
ISBN Egyptian edition 0 19 435083 5

Illustrations by David Lock,
Heather Clarke, Pythia Ashton-Jewell, Oxford Illustrators

Children's artwork by Bonnie Mylrea Lowndes and Thomas Mylrea Lowndes

Photographs by Brighton Borough Council Arts and Leisure Services (p. 69), Hazel Geatches (pp. 49, 69, 72),
Ray Geatches (p. 49), Angela Lilley (p. 88), Rachel Strachan (p. 49), Ruth Went (p. 72).

Designed and typeset by Oxprint Design, Oxford

Printed in Hong Kong

① Listen and read

1 It's quarter to eight. It's Monday morning. It's the first day of school. Adam's sleeping.

2 It's eight o'clock. Adam's putting on his clothes. He's got his socks but he can't find his shoes.

Get up, Adam.

Where are my shoes?

3 It's quarter past eight. Helen and Edward are having breakfast with Mum. Adam's late for breakfast.

4 It's half past eight. Adam's brushing his teeth. Helen's waiting for him. She's ready for school.

Don't touch Adam's juice, Edward.

Hurry up, Adam.

5 It's quarter to nine. Adam and Helen are going to school. Helen likes school.

6 Edward isn't going to school. He's only three. Edward's playing with Echo.

Hello, Sally.

Go away, Edward.

1

Workbook page

1

2 Ask and answer

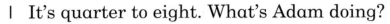

He's sleeping.

1 It's quarter to eight. What's Adam doing?
2 It's eight o'clock. Is Edward putting on his clothes?
3 It's quarter past eight. What's Mum doing?
4 It's half past eight. Is Helen waiting for Adam?
5 It's quarter to nine. What's Adam doing?
6 It's quarter to nine. Is Edward playing with Echo?

No, he isn't.

3 Ask and answer

It's ten o'clock.
Is Mum making a cake?

No, she isn't.

It's quarter to eleven.
What's Edward doing?

He's ___

4 Listen and say

She's washing the dishes, she's washing the
dishes, she's washing the dishes, she's
washing the dishes, she's washing the dishes

5 Listen and sing

Come in, close the door.
Sit on your chair,
And not on the floor.
Don't sit, don't sit
On the floor.

Where are we today?
We're at school, we're at school.
So let's smile and say
'We're at school, we're at school.
Hip, hip, hip, hooray!'

Listen, read and look.
Point at the board,
And not at your book.
Don't point, don't point
At your book.

camel

Where are we today? ...

Stand up, count to ten.
Write with a pencil,
And not with a pen.
Don't write, don't write
With a pen.

Where are we today? ...

6 Your game

1 Stand up!

2 Don't open your book!

Workbook
page
3

7 Listen and read 📼

1 Adam's now nine. He's now in Class 3 at Wilton Primary School. This year his teacher's Mrs Bell. Today's the first day of school.

2 Adam's got a pencil, a rubber, a ruler and a notebook in his bag. He's got his sandwiches and drink too. Adam's ready for school.

3 Adam likes art. He can draw and paint.

4 Adam can write stories too. He likes English. Art and English are his favourite subjects.

8 Ask and answer

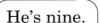

1 How old's Adam?
  He's nine.
2 Which class is he in?
3 Who's his teacher?

4 What's he got in his bag?
5 Which subjects does he like?
6 What can he do?

9 Your work

me

my teacher

I'm now nine.
I'm now in
class 3 at Bridge
Street School.

1 Listen and say

What's the time?
It's half past two.
Half past two.
Let's go to the zoo.

What's the time?
It's quarter to three.
Quarter to three.
It's time for tea.

What's the time?
It's five past four.
Five past four.
Please close the door.

What's the time?
It's ten to eight.
Ten to eight.
We mustn't be late.

What's the time?
It's twenty past nine.
Twenty past nine.
And we're all fine.

What's the time?
It's twenty-five to ten.
Twenty-five to ten.
Let's start again.

Workbook page 5

2 Listen, read and say 📟

a

five past five

b

ten past five

c

twenty past five

d

twenty-five past five

e

twenty-five to six

f

twenty to six

g

ten to six

h

five to six

3 Ask, answer and say

What's the time?

clock d

It's four o'clock.

What time is it?

It's ___

4 Listen and read

1 Bill's a vet. He looks after animals when they're sick. Bill works in a zoo. He's got an office there.

2 It's nine o'clock in the morning. Bill's arriving at work. He arrives at work at nine o'clock every morning.

3 Bill has lunch at midday. It's midday now. Bill's having lunch.

4 At five o'clock in the afternoon Bill goes home. It's five o'clock now. Bill's going home.

5 It's eight o'clock in the evening. Bill's having dinner. He has dinner at eight o'clock every evening.

6 Bill goes to bed at eleven o'clock at night. It's eleven o'clock now. Bill's going to bed.

7 It's midnight. Bill goes to sleep at midnight. He's going to sleep now.

Workbook page 7

5 Listen, read and say

1. It's nine o'clock in the morning.

2. It's midday.

3. It's five o'clock in the afternoon.

4. It's eight o'clock in the evening.

5. It's eleven o'clock at night.

6. It's midnight.

6 Ask and answer about Bill

What's the time?

It's nine o'clock in the morning.

What's Bill doing?

He's arriving at work. He arrives at work at nine every morning.

7 Your work

It's ten past eight in the morning. I'm brushing my teeth. I brush my teeth every morning.

UNIT 3

1 Listen and say

MUM	Hello, Adam. Did you have a good day at school?
ADAM	Yes, it was great! We had art and English.
MUM	What did you do in art?
ADAM	We painted pictures. I painted a seaside picture.
MUM	What about you, Helen? Did you have a good day?
HELEN	It was all right. We had maths. I'm not very good at maths.
ADAM	What did you do today, Mum?
MUM	I stayed at home. In the morning I washed the clothes. Then I cooked the lunch. In the afternoon I cleaned the house.
ADAM	What an awful day! What about Edward? Did he have a good day?
MUM	Yes, he did. He had a very good day.
ADAM	What did he do?
MUM	He played all morning and fell asleep after lunch!

2 Listen, read and say

1

fantastic
great
very good

2

all right
not bad
OK

3

awful
boring
terrible

Workbook
page
9

3 Ask and answer

Did you have a good day, Sally?

No, it was awful.

1	2	3	4	5	6

4 Listen, read and say

cleaned played stayed	cooked washed	painted

5 Ask and answer

What did Sally do?

She stayed in bed.

1

2

3

4

5

6

6 Listen and read

1 There are six monkeys at Bill's zoo. Minnie's the youngest. She's a baby.

2 Yesterday morning the zookeeper fed the monkeys. He put vegetables and nuts in a bowl. The monkeys ran to the bowl.

3 But Minnie didn't run to the bowl. Poor Minnie was sick.

4 The zookeeper called Minnie's name. But she didn't look up.

5 The zookeeper gave Minnie a carrot. But she didn't eat it. He gave her some nuts. But she didn't eat them.

6 The zookeeper took Minnie to Bill's office. Bill gave her some medicine. She had some milk too.

7 At five o'clock Bill wanted to go home. But poor Minnie was sick. So Bill took Minnie home with him.

8 Minnie isn't sick today. She's at Bill's house. She's very happy!

7 Listen, read and say

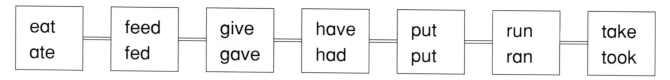

eat	feed	give	have	put	run	take
ate	fed	gave	had	put	ran	took

Workbook
page
11

8 Complete the sentences

The zookeeper fed the monkeys yesterday morning.

1 The zookeeper ___ the monkeys yesterday morning.
2 He ___ vegetables and nuts in a bowl.
3 Minnie ___ to the bowl.
4 The zookeeper ___ Minnie a carrot.
5 Minnie ___ the carrot.
6 She ___ some medicine.
7 The zookeeper ___ Minnie home with him.

fed / didn't feed
put / didn't put
ran / didn't run
gave / didn't give
ate / didn't eat
had / didn't have
took / didn't take

9 Ask and answer

1 Did the zookeeper feed the monkeys?
2 Did Minnie run to the bowl?
3 Did the zookeeper call Minnie's name?
4 Did Minnie eat the nuts?
5 Did Bill give Minnie some milk?
6 Did he go home?
7 Did Minnie stay at the zoo?

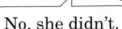

Yes, he did.

No, she didn't.

10 YOUR QUIZ ???????????????????

What did you do yesterday?

1 Did you paint a picture?
2 Did you have maths?
3 Did you wash your hands?
4 Did you play with your friends?
5 Did you stay at home?

6 Did you eat vegetables?
7 Did you have some milk?
8 Did you go to the park?
9 Did you listen to music?
10 Did you watch TV?

UNIT 4

1 Listen and read

1 Yesterday was Minnie's first day at Bill's house. Bill went to the zoo. Minnie stayed at home.

2 When Bill went to work, Minnie was bored. She wanted to play.

3 Minnie found a friend. She played with her friend. Minnie was happy.

4 Then Minnie's friend went away. Minnie was sad.

5 After that Minnie wanted something to eat. She was hungry.

6 She wanted something to drink because she was thirsty too.

7 Minnie was cold. She put on Bill's jumper.

8 It was a heavy jumper. Minnie took off the jumper because she was hot.

9 Minnie was tired when Bill got home. Bill was angry. 'Oh, Minnie,' he said, 'you are a naughty monkey.'

2 True or false?

1 Bill stayed at home yesterday. false
2 He played with Minnie.
3 Bill gave Minnie something to eat.
4 She had something to drink too.

13

Workbook page 13

3 Listen, read and say 😀

1 angry
2 bored
3 cold
4 happy
5 hot
6 hungry
7 naughty
8 sad
9 thirsty
10 tired

4 Complete the sentences

Minnie was bored because Bill went to work.

1 Minnie was ___ because Bill went to work.
2 She was ___ because she found a friend.
3 She was ___ because her friend went away.
4 She wanted something to eat because she was ___
5 She wanted something to drink because she was ___
6 She put on Bill's jumper because she was ___
7 She took off the jumper because she was ___

5 Your game

⬭bored⬭	happy	❌cold
hot	hungry	naughty
❌sad	thirsty	⬭tired⬭

Minnie was bored.

She was cold.

She was bored and tired.

She was cold and ___

6 Listen and read

My Weekend

Saturday

① Helen and I wanted to go to the park but it was cloudy and wet. In the morning we stayed at home. We were bored. We watched cartoons on TV. They were OK.

② In the afternoon Mum took us to the shops. Edward was naughty. He wanted to play with a toy. The toys all fell down. Mum was angry.

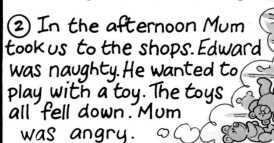

③ In the evening Helen and I did a jigsaw. Edward wanted to help. The jigsaw fell on to the floor. Helen was angry.

④ It was very windy at night. It rained. I didn't sleep very well. The wind was very noisy.

Sunday

⑤ On Sunday morning it was dry. It was hot and sunny too. Helen and I wanted to go to the park. But we didn't go to the park. We helped Dad in the garden. Dad was happy but we were tired.

⑥ In the afternoon Helen and I went to Sally's house. Sally was sick. She was in bed. She didn't want to play. Helen and I were sad.

⑦ In the evening it was cold and windy. But Helen and I wanted to go outside and play. So we put on our jumpers and took our kites to the park. We had a great time!

7 Read and say

1 He was happy. [e]
2 She was sick.
3 They were bored.
4 He was naughty.
5 She was tired.
6 They were angry.

 a
 b
 c
 d
 e
 f

8 Ask and answer

1 Was Edward naughty? Yes, he was.
2 Were Adam and Helen sick? No, they weren't.
3 Was Mum angry?
4 Were Adam and Helen tired?
5 Was Dad bored?
6 Were Adam and Helen sad?
7 Was Helen naughty?
8 Were Mum and Edward happy?

9   Your game

1 Listen and say

Workbook
page
19

② Listen, read and say

1 go riding

2 go swimming

3 go for a bike ride

4 go for a walk

5 go to the beach

6 go to the park

③ Ask and answer

Can I go to the beach?

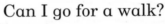

No, you can't.

Can I go for a walk?

Yes, all right.

1

2

3

4 PARK CLOSED

5

6

Workbook page 20

18

4 Listen and sing

Can I have a burger?
Please, Mum, please.
Can I have a burger?
I'm hungry.

You can have a burger.
Yes, all right.
But don't say your tummy hurts
In the night!

Can I have some milk?
Please, Dad, please.
Can I have some milk?
I'm thirsty.

You can have some milk.
Yes, all right.
But don't say your tummy hurts
In the night!

Can I have an apple?
Please, Mum, please.
Can I have an apple?
I'm hungry.

You can have an apple.
Yes, all right.
But don't say your tummy hurts
In the night!

Can I have some ... 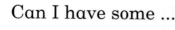   Can I have some ...   Can I have an ...

Can I have a ...   Can I have some ...   Can I have some ...

Workbook
page
21

5 Ask and answer

1

2

3

4

5

6

Can I borrow a pencil, please?

Yes, here you are.

Can I borrow a yellow crayon, please?

Sorry, I haven't got a yellow crayon.

6 Your game

1 Can I borrow a ruler, please?

Sorry, I haven't got a ruler.

2 Can I borrow a ruler, please?

Yes, here you are.

1 Listen and say

Bill's a happy worker.
Just look and see.
Bill's a happy worker.
He's working happily.

Bill's a quick reader.
Just look and see.
Bill's a quick reader.
He's reading quickly.

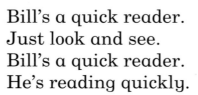

Bill's a careful driver.
Just look and see.
Bill's a careful driver.
He's driving carefully.

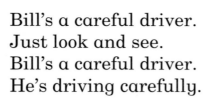

Bill's a slow eater.
Just look and see.
Bill's a slow eater.
He's eating slowly.

Bill's a quiet talker.
Just look and see.
Bill's a quiet talker.
He's talking quietly.

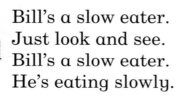

Bill's a loud singer.
Just look and see.
Bill's a loud singer.
He's singing loudly.

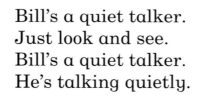

Minnie's only a monkey.
She can't read or talk.
She can't drive.
And she can't sing.
But she can eat and walk.

Workbook
page
23

2 Complete the sentences

1 Minnie ___ eat.
2 She ___ talk.
3 She ___ drive.
4 She ___ sing.
5 She ___ read.
6 She ___ walk.

Minnie can eat.

She can't talk.

3 Ask and answer

1 Can Minnie read?
2 Can Bill read?
3 Can Minnie talk?
4 Can Bill drive?
5 Can Minnie drive?
6 Can she walk?

No, she can't.

Yes, he can.

4 True or false?

1 Bill works happily.
2 He reads slowly.
3 He talks loudly.
4 He drives carefully.
5 He sings quietly.
6 He eats quickly.

true

5 Listen, read and say 😐

| careful | | happy | | loud | | quick | | quiet | | slow |
| carefully | | happily | | loudly | | quickly | | quietly | | slowly |

6 Read and say

1 He's listening carefully. (b)

2 She's playing happily.

3 He's talking loudly.

4 She's walking slowly.

5 He's running quickly.

6 She's sitting quietly.

23

Workbook page 25

7 Listen and sing

Sing this verse quietly.
One, two and three.
Sing this verse quietly.
Just listen to me.

I can sing quietly.
Just listen to me.
I can sing quietly.
It's easy, you see.

Sing this verse loudly.
One, two and three.
Sing this verse loudly.
Just listen to me.

I can sing loudly.
Just listen to me.
I can sing loudly.
It's easy, you see.

Sing this verse slowly.
One, two and three.
Sing this verse slowly.
Just listen to me.

I can sing slowly.
Just listen to me.
I can sing slowly.
It's easy, you see.

Sing this verse quickly.
One, two and three.
Sing this verse quickly.
Just listen to me.

I can sing quickly.
Just listen to me.
I can sing quickly.
It's easy, you see.

8 Your game

1 Stand up.

2 Stand up quickly.

Workbook page 26

1 Listen and read

I always have cereal for breakfast. I have it with milk and sugar. I usually have juice too. Sometimes I have milk.

1

2

Mum never has cereal. She doesn't like cereal or milk. She always has toast and jam. She drinks coffee for breakfast.

Dad usually has an egg on toast. When he's late for work, he has toast and jam. Dad doesn't like coffee. He drinks tea for breakfast.

3

4

Edward often has fruit for breakfast. Bananas are his favourite. He sometimes has a biscuit too. He doesn't like cereal.

Helen likes fruit too. She usually has an apple or an orange and a bread roll and jam. She usually has tea to drink.

5

6

Tabby always has cat food and milk – for breakfast, lunch and dinner!

Echo likes fruit and nuts. He's a naughty parrot. He likes my food too!

7

Workbook
page
27

2 Listen, read and say 📼

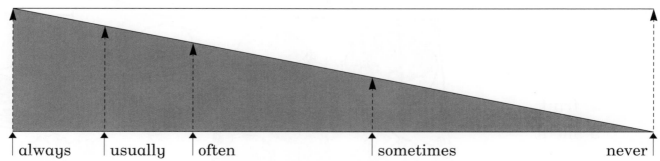

always	usually	often	sometimes	never

3 Say and point

Sally never has a bread roll for breakfast.

	always	usually	often	sometimes	never
🍞		✔			
🍲				✔	
🍳					✔
🧇				✔	
🥖					✔
🍎🍊🍌			✔		
🥛		✔			
☕					✔
🍵	✔				
🧃🥛					✔

4 Listen and say 📼

A bread roll for breakfast, a bread roll for breakfast,
a bread roll for breakfast, a bread roll for breakfast

5 **Read and say**

1 bread ⟨ c ⟩
2 cheese
3 fish
4 fruit
5 meat
6 rice
7 salad

8 chips
9 grapes
10 vegetables

11 a burger
12 an omelette
13 a pizza

6 **Your game**

Workbook page 29

HOW HEALTHY ARE YOU?

True or false?

1 I like milk and fruit juice.

2 I don't have chips every day.

3 I have fish or chicken every week.

4 I don't like burgers.

5 I like sport and swimming.

Complete the sentences

6 I ___ go to bed before eight o'clock.

7 I ___ sleep for ten hours.

8 I ___ have breakfast before school.

9 I ___ walk to school.

10 I ___ play outside after school.

8 Your work

This is what I have for my meals.

I usually have bread and jam for breakfast. I have juice too.

I have lunch at school. I usually have a cheese sandwich and a cake. I usually have cola to drink.

For dinner I have meat and rice. After that I have fruit. Sometimes I have ice cream.

UNIT 8

1 Listen and say

1 Oh, no! My kite's broken.

2 Can you mend my kite, Dad?
Sorry, I can't. I'm watering the plants.

3 Can you mend my kite, Helen?
Sorry, I can't. I'm doing my homework.

4 Can you mend my kite, Mum?
Sorry, I can't. I'm making the dinner.

5 Oh, dear! Come on, Echo. Let's have a look at this kite.

6 Adam! Dinner's nearly ready. Can you lay the table?
Sorry, Mum. I can't lay the table because I'm mending my kite!

2 Read and say

1 He's mending his kite. (c)
2 She's making the dinner.
3 He's watering the plants.
4 She's doing her homework.
5 He's helping Adam.

29

Workbook page 31

3 Listen, read and say 🔲

1 feed the cat

2 lay the table

3 make your bed

4 put your clothes away

5 tidy your room

6 wash the dishes

4 Your game

1
Can you feed the cat?
Sorry, I can't. I'm laying the table.

2
Can you wash the dishes?
Yes, all right.

Workbook page 32

⑤ Listen, read and say 📷

bathroom	bedroom	garage	garden	kitchen	living room

⑥ Ask and answer

Where's Helen?

She's in the kitchen.

What's she doing?

She's making a sandwich.

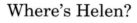

⑦ Ask and answer

Can you help me, Helen?

Sorry, I can't. I'm making a sandwich.

Can you help me, Edward?

Sorry, I can't. I'm ___

31

Workbook page 33

8 Listen and say 📼

Can you put your books away?
Then we can go and play.
Pick your books up from the floor.
Put them in the cupboard.
And close the door.

Can you put your kite away?
Then we can go and play.
Pick your kite up from the floor.
Put it in the cupboard.
And close the drawer.

9 Your game

1

Close the door.
Water the plants.
Wash the dishes.
Make the lunch.

2

Close the door.
Water the plants.
Wash the dishes.
Make the lunch.

Can you close the door?

Can you water the plants?

3

Sorry, I can't.

Close the door.
plants.
Wash the dishes.
Make the lunch.

4

Close the door. ✗
Water the plants.
Wash the dishes.
Make the lunch.

Water the plants

Yes, all right.

Workbook page 34

1 Listen and say

1 Hello. Can I help you?

Yes, please. I'd like a fishburger and a beefburger.

2 A fishburger and a beefburger. Here you are. Would you like some chips?

Yes, please. Two bags.

3 Would you like an ice cream? We've got banana, chocolate and strawberry.

No, thank you. I'd like two apple pies.

4 What would you like to drink?

Some coffee, please. And some lemonade.

5 Would you like a tray?

I'd like two trays, please.

6 Beefburger, chips, apple pie, lemonade.

7 Here you are, Minnie. Here's your lunch.

2 Read and match

What would you like to eat?  I'd like a beefburger and chips, please.

1 What would you like to eat?
2 What would you like to drink?
3 Would you like an ice cream?
4 Would you like some coffee?

a Yes, please. I'd like a chocolate ice cream.
b I'd like a beefburger and chips, please.
c I'd like some coffee, please.
d No, thank you. I'd like some lemonade.

33

Workbook page 37

③ Read and say

1 a beefburger
2 a fishburger
3 a cheeseburger
4 some chips
5 an apple pie
6 a banana ice cream
7 a chocolate ice cream
8 a strawberry ice cream

9 some coffee
10 some tea
11 some lemonade
12 some orange juice

④ Ask and answer about you

What would you like to eat?

I'd like a cheeseburger, please.

Would you like an apple pie?

Yes, please.

⑤ Listen and say

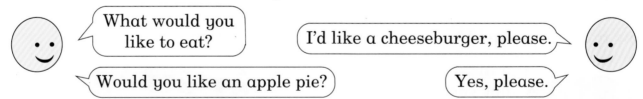

I'd like lemonade, I'd like lemonade, I'd like lemonade, I'd like lemonade, I'd like lemonade, I'd like lemonade, I'd like lemonade, I'd like lemonade

6 Listen and say 😐

I'd like some rice with my meat.
How much rice would you like to eat?
Not very much. Not a lot.
Just a little rice. That's what you've got.

I'd like some bread with my meat.
How much bread would you like to eat?
I like bread. I'd like a lot.
A lot of bread. That's what you've got.

I'd like some beans with my meat.
How many beans would you like to eat?
Not very many. Not a lot.
Just a few beans. That's what you've got.

I'd like some peas with my meat.
How many peas would you like to eat?
I like peas. I'd like a lot.
A lot of peas. That's what you've got.

7 Listen, read and say 😐

How much chocolate?

1
a little
not very much
not a lot

How much chocolate?

2
a lot

How many sweets?

3
a few
not very many
not a lot

How many sweets?

4
a lot

Workbook
page
39

8 **Ask and answer**

How much pineapple would you like?

A lot, please. I like pineapple.

How many nuts would you like?

Just a few, please.

1   2   3   4

5   6   7   8

9 **Ask and answer about you**

How much pineapple would you like?

Just a little, please.

10 **Your work**

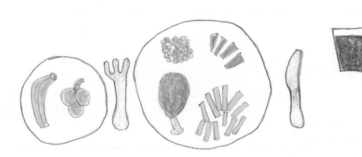

This is what I'd like for dinner this evening.

I'd like some meat with a few vegetables. I'd like some chips too. I'd like a lot of chips. After that I'd like some fruit. I'd like a few grapes and a banana. And I'd like some cola to drink.

1 Listen and read

1. What does Bill like doing in his free time?

2. He likes collecting stamps. He collects animal stamps.

3. He likes painting. He paints animal pictures.

4. He likes reading. He reads animal books.

5. He likes watching TV. He watches TV every day.

6. He likes riding. He rides once or twice a week.

7. He likes playing tennis. He plays tennis two or three times a month.

8. He goes on holiday once a year. He likes going on holiday. He likes going to zoos!

2 Complete the sentences

Bill collects animal stamps.

1	Bill collects ___	a	on holiday once a year.
2	He goes ___	b	animal books.
3	He plays ___	c	once or twice a week.
4	He reads ___	d	tennis two or three times a month.
5	He rides ___	e	animal stamps.
6	He watches ___	f	TV every day.

Workbook page 41

3 Ask and answer

Does Bill like doing gym?

Yes, he does.

Does he like running?

No, he doesn't.

4 Ask and answer about you

Do you like doing gym?

Do you like running?

No, I don't.

Yes, I do.

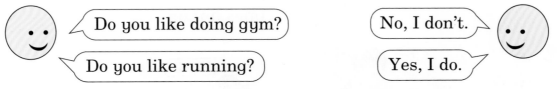

5 Listen and say

Do you like skipping?
Yes, I do.
I like skipping.
I like it too.

Do you like jumping?
Yes, I do.
I like jumping.
I like it too.

Workbook
page
42

6 Listen, read and say 😐

1 every day

2 once a week

Monday
Tuesday
Wednesday
Thursday
Friday
Saturday
Sunday

3 twice a month

4 three times a year

7 Say and point

Sally visits Adam and Helen two or three times a month.

1

three or four times a month

2

every day

3

two or three times a month

4

once a week

5
two or three times a year

6
once a week

7

twice a month

8

two or three times a year

9

three or four times a week

10

every day

8 Ask and answer about you

Do you do karate?

Do you listen to music?

No, I don't.

Yes, I do. I listen to music every day.

9 Your work

In my free time I play with my friends. I like playing games. I like going to the cinema and watching TV too. I go to the cinema once or twice a month. I watch TV every day.

UNIT 11

1 Listen and say

2 Complete the sentences

The children must put on their helmets.

1 The children ___ put on their helmets.
2 They ___ ride in the road.
3 They ___ be careful.
4 They ___ be late.

Workbook
page
45

③ Listen, read and say 😐

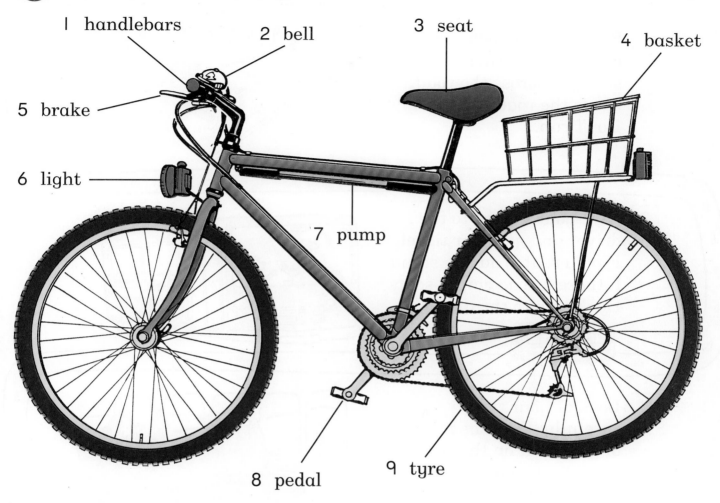

1 handlebars
2 bell
3 seat
4 basket
5 brake
6 light
7 pump
8 pedal
9 tyre

④ Read and say

1 You must hold the handlebars. (e)
2 You must have lights.
3 You must put your things in your basket.
4 You mustn't stand on the seat.
5 Your feet must touch the pedals.
6 You mustn't sit on the handlebars.
7 You must pump your tyres.

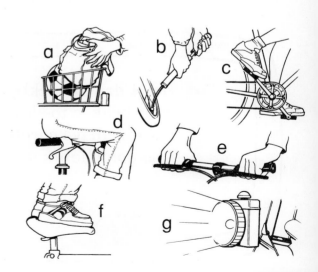

a
b
c
d
e
f
g

Workbook page
46

5 **Listen and read**

1 Stop and look before you cross a road. Then walk straight across the road. Cross the road quickly. Don't run.

2 Give your money to the driver and get your ticket. Find a seat. You can stand if there are no empty seats. Don't talk to the driver.

3 Look at your ticket carefully. Find the number of your seat on the ticket. Then find your seat. Put your bag under your seat. Sit down quickly.

4 Don't drive quickly. Use your brakes to slow down. Always drive carefully. Use your lights at night.

Workbook page 47

6 **Listen, read and say** 🔲

1
by bus

2
by car

3
by plane

4
on foot

7 **Complete the sentences**

> You must use your lights at night when you travel by car.

1 You must use your lights at night ___
2 You mustn't run across the road ___
3 You must look at your ticket carefully ___
4 You mustn't talk to the driver ___
5 You must get a ticket from the driver ___
6 You mustn't drive quickly ___
7 You must cross the road quickly ___
8 You must look before you cross ___
9 You must sit down quickly ___
10 You must drive carefully ___

8 **Your work**

You mustn't walk in the road.

You mustn't ride bikes.

Workbook
page
48

44

1 Listen and read

1 It was Saturday yesterday. Adam and his family went shopping.

2 Helen went with Dad. Dad took the car to the petrol station to get some petrol.

3 Then they went to the library. Helen got some new books.

4 First Mum went to the supermarket to buy some food. Adam and Edward went with her.

5 Then they went to the hairdresser's. Adam got a haircut.

6 After that they went to the toyshop. Edward wanted a new toy. Mum bought him a cowboy hat.

7 Finally they went to a restaurant. Dad and Helen were there. They had a pizza.

2 Ask and answer

1 Why did Dad go to the petrol station?
2 Why did Helen go to the library?
3 Why did Mum go to the supermarket?
4 Why did Adam go to the hairdresser's?
5 Why did Edward go to the toyshop?

To get some petrol.

To ___

Workbook page 49

3 **Listen, read and say** 😐

1 baker's

2 butcher's

3 chemist's

4 greengrocer's

5 newsagent's

6 post office

4 **Ask and answer**

Why did Mum go to the baker's?  To get some bread rolls.

meat

vegetables

stamps

toothbrush

bread rolls

newspaper

Workbook page 50

5 Listen and sing

There's a hole in my bucket, dear Liza, dear Liza.
There's a hole in my bucket, dear Liza, a hole.

   Then mend it, dear Henry, dear Henry, dear Henry.
   Then mend it, dear Henry, dear Henry, mend it.

How can I mend it, dear Liza, dear Liza?
How can I mend it, dear Liza, how?

   With straw, dear Henry, dear Henry, dear Henry.
   With straw, dear Henry, dear Henry, with straw.

But the straw's too long, dear Liza ...

   Then cut it, dear Henry ...

How can I cut it, dear Liza ...

   With a knife, dear Henry ...

But the knife's too blunt, dear Liza ...

   Then sharpen it, dear Henry ...

How can I sharpen it, dear Liza ...

   With a stone, dear Henry ...

But the stone's too dry, dear Liza ...

   Then wet it, dear Henry ...

How can I wet it, dear Liza ...

   With water, dear Henry ...

How can I fetch it, dear Liza ...

   In a bucket, dear Henry ...

There's a hole in my bucket, dear Liza ...

Workbook
page
51

6 Listen, read and say 📷

1 a bucket

2 a knife

3 a stone

4 some straw

5 some water

7 Ask and answer

Why does Henry need a bucket?

To fetch some water.

Why does he need a knife?

To ___

8 YOUR QUIZ ????????????????

1 Why do you go to the seaside?

2 Why do you go to the cinema?

3 Why do you go to the hospital?

4 Why do you go to the hotel?

5 Why do you go to the swimming pool?

6 Why do you go to the park?

7 Why do you go to the restaurant?

8 Why do you go to the station?

9 Why do you go to the museum?

10 Why do you go to the zoo?

Workbook
page
52

1 Listen and read 🔲

The Seasons in Britain

1

In winter the weather's cold and wet. It rains a lot and it sometimes snows. The sun doesn't shine very much in winter. It's often cloudy.

2

The weather's warmer in spring. It's sunnier too. It's sometimes wet.

3

Summer's the hottest season. It's hotter than spring. The sun usually shines every day. It doesn't usually rain. It's usually dry.

4

In autumn the days are cool and wet. The sky's often grey and cloudy. It's often windy too. It doesn't snow in autumn but it rains a lot.

2 Listen, read and say 🔲

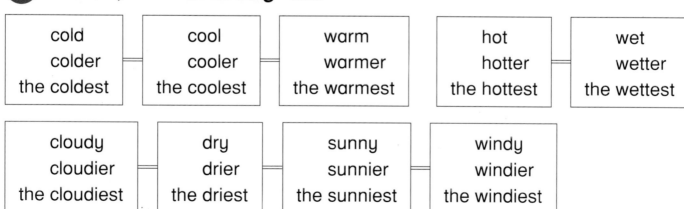

cold	cool	warm	hot	wet
colder	cooler	warmer	hotter	wetter
the coldest	the coolest	the warmest	the hottest	the wettest

cloudy	dry	sunny	windy
cloudier	drier	sunnier	windier
the cloudiest	the driest	the sunniest	the windiest

Workbook page 55

3 Complete the sentences

 Winter is colder than autumn and spring.

1 ___ is colder than autumn and spring.
2 ___ and winter are wetter than spring.
3 Spring is warmer and sunnier than ___
4 Autumn and spring are cooler than ___
5 ___ is hotter and drier than spring.
6 ___ is cloudier and windier than summer.

Summer / Winter
Autumn / Summer
summer / winter
summer / winter
Summer / Winter
Autumn / Spring

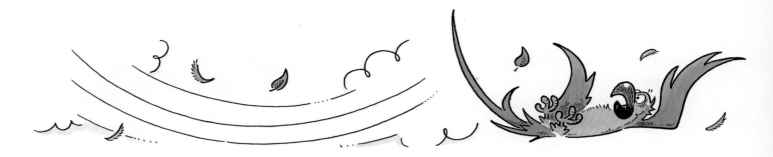

4 Complete the sentences

1 The coldest season's ___
2 ___ and ___ are the wettest seasons.
3 The driest and hottest season's ___
4 ___'s the windiest season.
5 The sunniest season's ___

The coldest season's winter.

5 Listen and say

The sunniest season's summer, the sunniest season's summer, the sunniest season's summer, the sunniest season's summer, the sunniest season's summer, the

Workbook
page
56

50

6 Listen and read 📼

THE **WIND** AND THE **SUN**

*O*ne autumn day, high up in the sky, the wind met the sun. The wind and the sun were not good friends.

'I'm stronger than you,' the wind said.

'No, you aren't,' the sun said. 'I'm stronger.'

'You aren't stronger,' the wind said. 'I know you aren't.'

'Can you see that park down there?' the sun asked. 'Can you see that man with the umbrella? The man with the heavy coat? I can remove his coat but you can't.'

'I can remove his coat,' the wind said. 'Watch me! I can blow it off.'

'OK,' the sun said. 'I'm watching.'

The wind started to blow. It blew and blew. But the man's coat didn't come off. It was very windy. The man got colder and colder. He put on his hat and his gloves. He wrapped his scarf around his neck. He fastened his coat.

Next it was the sun's turn. The sun started to shine. It got warmer. The man got warmer. The sun shone strongly. The man took off his hat and his gloves. Then he unwrapped his scarf. After that he unfastened his coat and took it off.

Did the wind remove the man's coat?
Or did the sun? Was the wind stronger?
Or was the sun?

Workbook
page
57

7 **Listen, read and say**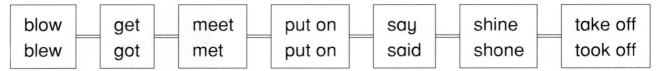

blow	get	meet	put on	say	shine	take off
blew	got	met	put on	said	shone	took off

8 **Put the sentences in order**

1   The wind met the sun.

2   ___

a   The sun started to shine.

b   The wind met the sun.

c   The sun removed the man's coat.

d   The man got warmer.

e   The wind started to blow.

f   The man got colder.

9 **Your work**

My favourite season's summer.

Summer is my favourite season. The weather is hot and dry. In summer I play in the garden. Sometimes I go to the beach with my mum and dad. I like summer.

1 Listen and say

BILL   Hello, Kate. It's Bill. How are you?

KATE   I'm fine, thanks.

BILL   I've got a pet. Her name's Minnie. She's a monkey. Why don't you come and see her?

KATE   That's a good idea. I'm on holiday next week.

BILL   Oh, good!

KATE   I can't come on Monday. I'm going to the hairdresser's.

BILL   What about Tuesday?

KATE   On Tuesday I'm visiting Gran.

BILL   What are you doing on Wednesday?

KATE   I'm playing tennis with some friends.

BILL   What about Thursday, then?

KATE   I'm busy on Thursday too. I'm going shopping on Thursday.

BILL   Can you come on Friday, then?

KATE   I'm sorry, I can't. I'm going to the cinema.

BILL   You're very busy, Kate. What about ...

        Oh, Minnie. You are a naughty monkey!

2 Complete the sentences

1 Kate's going to the cinema on ___

2 She's playing tennis on ___

3 She's going shopping on ___

4 She's going to the hairdresser's on ___

5 She's visiting her gran on ___

Kate's going to the cinema on Friday.

Workbook page 59

3 Ask and answer

1 Is Kate going to the cinema on Tuesday?
2 Is she visiting her grandmother on Tuesday?
3 Is she playing tennis on Friday?
4 Is she playing tennis on Wednesday?
5 Is she going shopping on Monday?
6 Is she going to the cinema on Friday?
7 Is she going to the hairdresser's on Thursday?
8 Is she visiting her grandmother on Wednesday?
9 Is she going shopping on Thursday?
10 Is she going to the hairdresser's on Monday?

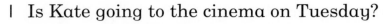

No, she isn't.

Yes, she is.

4 Ask and answer

What's Bill doing on Monday?

He's going for a bike ride.

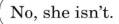

MONDAY
bike ride with Jeff

TUESDAY
doctor's – 6.30

WEDNESDAY
riding

THURSDAY
~~riding~~ swimming

FRIDAY
volleyball – club, 7 o'clock

SATURDAY
visiting London – meet Kate 9.30

SUNDAY
Mrs Green – lunch

Workbook page 61

55

6 **Your conversation**

Let's go to the zoo on Tuesday.

What about Friday?

What about Sunday?

I'm busy on Tuesday. I'm going to the doctor's.

I can't on Friday. I'm going skating.

That's a good idea. Let's go to the zoo on Sunday.

7 **Your work**

This is what I'm doing next week.

On Monday I'm visiting my grandmother and grandfather. I'm going to a birthday party on Wednesday. It's my cousin's birthday. On Saturday I'm going shopping with my mum and dad.

UNIT 15

1 Listen and say 😐

MRS GREEN	Hello, Bill.
BILL	Hello, Mrs Green. Can I help you?
MRS GREEN	Is your monkey here?
BILL	Minnie? I think she's here. Why?
MRS GREEN	Well, Minnie came into my house today.
BILL	Oh, I'm sorry, Mrs Green. Minnie's a naughty monkey. How did she get in?
MRS GREEN	She climbed in through the window. She took some of my jewellery.
BILL	What did she take?
MRS GREEN	She took my favourite earrings. I usually put them in a cupboard. But I didn't put them away last night.
BILL	Where did she find them?
MRS GREEN	On the living room table. She came in and picked up the earrings. Then she climbed out through the window again.
BILL	When did Minnie do this?
MRS GREEN	This morning, after you went to work.
BILL	Oh dear, Mrs Green. I am sorry. Let's go and find Minnie.
	Oh, Minnie. You are a naughty monkey.

Workbook
page
63

2 Ask and answer

1 Did Mrs Green put away her earrings last night?
2 Did she put them in the cupboard?
3 Did Minnie go into Mrs Green's house last night?
4 Did she take some jewellery?
5 Did Bill go into Mrs Green's house?

No, she didn't.

3 Listen, read and say

1 bracelet

2 earrings

3 necklace

4 ring

4 Read and match

When did Minnie go into Mrs Green's house?

After Bill went to work.

1 When did Minnie go into Mrs Green's house?
2 What did she do there?
3 How did she get out?
4 Where did Mrs Green put her earrings?
5 What did Minnie take?

a She climbed out through the window.
b She picked up some of Mrs Green's jewellery.
c On the table.
d Mrs Green's earrings, bracelet, necklace and ring.
e After Bill went to work.

Workbook page 64

5 Listen and read

Bill's sister, Kate, went to London yesterday. Bill lives in London. Kate wanted to meet Bill's pet, Minnie the monkey. This is what Kate did yesterday.

Kate got up at half past seven. Before breakfast she had a shower. Then she put on her clothes and brushed her hair. After breakfast she brushed her teeth. Then she put on her coat and went to the station and got on a train. Bill met her at the station in London. Minnie didn't go to the station. She stayed at home.

Kate wanted to see Minnie. She wanted to do lots of things in London too. First Bill and Kate went to the Science Museum. Then they went shopping. They bought some sandwiches. Kate bought a bracelet, some earrings, a necklace and a ring. They ate the sandwiches in a park.

In the afternoon Bill and Kate went on a boat. They enjoyed it a lot. After that Kate wanted to meet Minnie. They went to Bill's house and Kate met Minnie.

Kate played with Minnie. They played with Minnie's ball. Then Kate fed Minnie. Before she left, she gave Minnie some presents. Minnie was very pleased!

Bill and Minnie took Kate to the station. Her train left at twenty past six. When she got home, she had dinner. At ten o'clock she went to bed. Before she got into bed, Kate looked in her bag. And what did she find? In her bag she found a present – Minnie's ball!

Workbook page 65

6 Ask and answer

1 How did Kate go to London?
2 Where did she go in the morning?
3 What did she buy?
4 When did she go to Bill's house?
5 What time did her train leave?
6 What did she find in her bag?

She went by train.

7 Complete the sentences

When did Kate brush her hair?

1 ___ did Kate brush her hair?   Before breakfast.
2 ___ did she do at the station?   She got on a train.
3 ___ did she eat her sandwiches?   In a park.
4 ___ did she go on a boat trip?   In the afternoon.
5 ___ did she give Minnie?   Some presents.
6 ___ did Kate go home?   On a train.

8 Your work

This is what I did yesterday. After breakfast I went
to school. After lunch we had English and music.
My teacher played the piano. In the evening I had
dinner and watched television. Then I went to bed.

UNIT 16

1 Listen and say

1. I like animal programmes. They're interesting.

2. Sports programmes are interesting too.

3. Films are OK. They're more interesting than the news.

4. I don't like the news. It's boring.

5. Music programmes are boring too.

6. Quiz shows are very boring. They're the most boring programmes on TV.

7. I like cartoons best. They're on TV every day. I watch them with my friends.

2 Listen, read and say

1. cartoon

2. film

3. the news

4. quiz show

5. animal programme

6. music programme

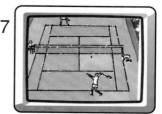

7. sports programme

Workbook page

67

3 Ask and answer about you

Do you like the news?

Do you like quiz shows?

No, I don't. It's boring.

Yes, I do. They're interesting.

4 Listen, read and say

boring	interesting
more boring	more interesting
the most boring	the most interesting

Quiz shows are more boring than animal programmes.

5 Say and point

boring	more boring	the most boring

Films are the most interesting.

interesting	more interesting	the most interesting

6 Listen and read

I
2

I like Music Box. It's my favourite programme on TV. Music Box is on twice a week. It's on Mondays and Thursdays at seven o'clock in the evening. It's on Channel 2. There are lots of singers on Music Box. I like listening to their songs and watching their videos. I watch Pop World on Channel 4 too. It's on Saturday evening. There are no videos on Pop World. I think Music Box is better.

My favourite programme on TV is Animal Magic. It's on Channel 1. It's on Saturdays at half past four in the afternoon. I sometimes watch it with Minnie. I watch Animal Life too. It's on Channel 3 on Sundays at two o'clock in the afternoon.

7 Read and match

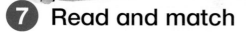

What's Music Box?　　It's a music programme.

1 What's Music Box?	a It's on Channel 2.
2 Which channel's it on?	b It's a music programme.
3 What time's it on?	c It's at seven o'clock.
4 What day's it on?	d It's on Mondays and Thursdays.

Workbook
page
69

8 Ask and answer

What's Animal Magic?

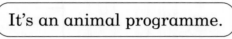

It's an animal programme.

Which channel's it on?

It's ___

9 YOUR TELEVISION QUIZ ?????????????

1 Have you got a TV at home?

2 Do you like watching TV?

3 Are quiz shows interesting?

4 Did you watch a film last week?

5 What's your favourite programme?

6 Is it a cartoon?

7 Which channel's it on?

8 What day's it on?

9 What time's it on?

10 Your work

My favourite Programme

My favourite programme is sport on Saturday. I watch it every week with my brother. It's on Saturdays at half past three in the afternoon. I like watching the football best. My brother likes the tennis.

UNIT 17

1 Listen and read

1 Today is Saturday. Bill isn't at work. He's at the station. Minnie's with him. He's got his ticket.

2 Bill's going to get onto the train.

3 Bill's got a map with him. He's going to look at his map.

4 The train's stopping. Bill's going to get off.

5 Bill's walking in the country. It's a long walk.

6 Bill's getting tired. He's going to go into this café and have a cup of tea.

7 Now Bill's going to walk back to the station.

8 Oh no! It's going to rain. Bill hasn't got his umbrella with him. He's going to get wet!

9 Bill's getting wet. Next Saturday he's going to stay at home!

2 Put the sentences about Bill in order

> 1 He buys a ticket.

a He looks at his map.

b He buys a ticket.

c He gets off the train.

d He gets wet.

e He gets on the train.

f He has a cup of tea.

65

Workbook page 73

3 Read and say

1 He's going to have a bath. 【d】
2 He's going to dry his clothes.
3 He's going to have dinner.
4 He's going to wash the dishes.
5 He's going to watch TV.
6 He's going to go to bed.

a
b

c
d
e
f

4 Say and point

He's going to make some biscuits.

1
2
3

4
5
6

Workbook page 74

5 Listen and read

A man's going for a walk.
Oh, no! It's going to rain.
The man hasn't got a hat.
He hasn't got an umbrella.
His clothes are going to get wet.
His shoes are going to get wet.
But his hair isn't going to get wet.

Who is the man? Is it Tom, Dick or Harry?

TOM   DICK   HARRY

6 Complete the sentences

1 Tom's hair isn't going to get wet ___

2 Dick's hair is going to get wet ___

3 Harry's hair isn't going to get wet ___

a because he hasn't got any hair.

b because he's got an umbrella.

c because he hasn't got an umbrella.

7 Ask and answer

1 Are Tom's clothes going to get wet?

2 Is Dick's hair going to get wet?

3 Are Tom's shoes going to get wet?

4 Are Dick's clothes going to get wet?

5 Is Tom's hair going to get wet?

6 Are Dick's shoes going to get wet?

No, they aren't.

Yes, it is.

Workbook page
75

8 Listen, read and say

1
I'm going to get wet.

2
I'm getting wet.

3
I got wet.

9 Your game

I'm at the club.

I'm at the club. I'm going to play tennis.

I'm at the club. I'm going to play tennis and I'm going to do judo.

I'm at the club. I'm going to play tennis, I'm going to do judo and I'm going to go swimming.

Workbook page 76

68

UNIT 18

1 Listen and read

1

Bill's going on holiday for two weeks. Minnie's going with him. First Bill and Minnie are going to Bath. They're going to stay there three nights. They're going to stay in a hotel. They're going to go on a boat. And they're going to go to a museum.

2

Then they're going to Benson. They're going to stay there two nights. They're going to stay in a tent. They're going to go swimming in the river Thames. And they're going to go walking.

3

After that they're going to the country. They're going to stay four nights on a farm. They're going to collect the eggs and feed the animals.

4

Finally they're going to Brighton. They're going to stay five nights in a caravan. They're going to go to the beach and the circus.

69

Workbook page 77

2 Listen, read and say

1	2	3	4
in a caravan	on a farm	in a hotel	in a tent

3 Say and point

They're going to go to a museum.

4 Ask and answer

First Bill and Minnie are going to Bath.

1 Are they going to stay three nights?
2 Are they going to stay in a caravan?
3 Are they going to go on a boat?

Yes, they are.

Then they're going to Benson.

4 Are they going to stay four nights?
5 Are they going to stay in a tent?
6 Are they going to go to the beach?

5 Ask and answer

After that they're going to the country.

1 How long are they going to stay there?
2 Where are they going to stay?
3 What are they going to do?

They're going to stay four nights.

Finally they're going to Brighton.

4 How long are they going to stay there?
5 Where are they going to stay?
6 What are they going to do?

Workbook page
79

6 Your conversation

1 Where are Bill and Minnie going?

They're going to Cairo.

2 How long are they going to stay there?

_____

3 Where are they going to stay?

_____

4 What are they going to do?

_____

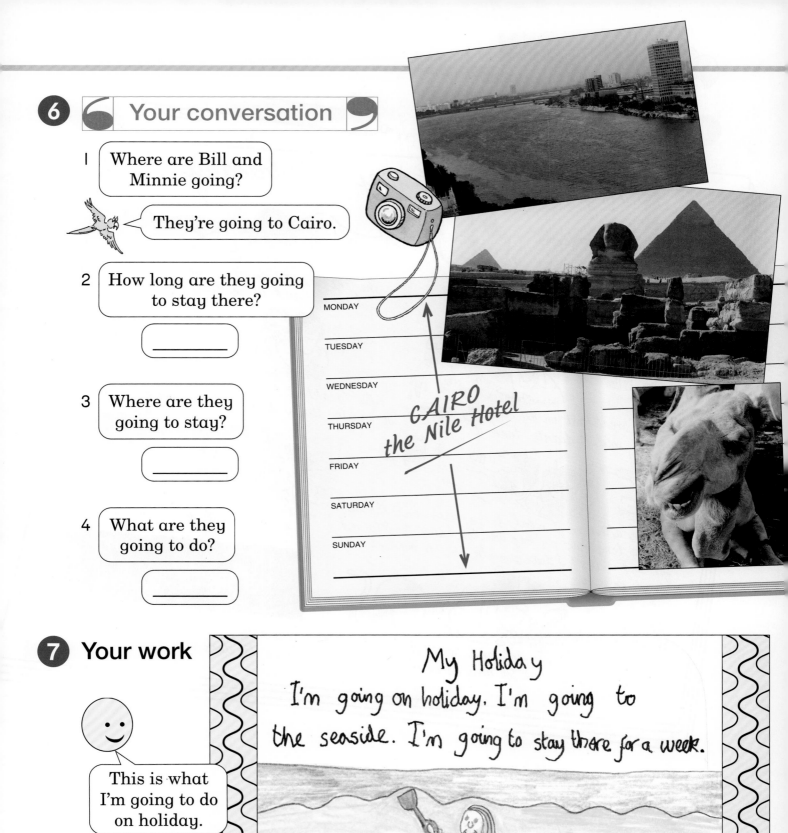

MONDAY

TUESDAY

WEDNESDAY

THURSDAY

FRIDAY

SATURDAY

SUNDAY

CAIRO
the Nile Hotel

7 Your work

This is what I'm going to do on holiday.

My Holiday
I'm going on holiday. I'm going to the seaside. I'm going to stay there for a week.

Workbook page 80

1 Listen and read 📺

My Holiday Diary – Wednesday

I slept badly. The ground was too hard. I like my bed at home. It's soft.

The tent was too small. Or am I too tall? I can't stand up in this tent.

I made breakfast on my stove. My coffee was too cold. I didn't drink it.

After breakfast I went swimming in the river. It was too deep. I didn't like swimming in it.

In the afternoon I went for a walk. But the walk was too long. And my bag was too heavy. Am I too old for long walks? I didn't walk back to my tent. I got on a bus!

In the evening I wanted to go to a restaurant. But it was too expensive.

I went back to my tent and cooked dinner. I didn't use my plate. It was too dirty. I used the pan.

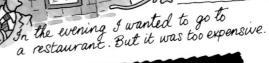

I didn't write my diary at night. It was too dark and I was too tired.

2 True or false?

1 Bill slept badly in his tent. (true)   4 He went for a walk.

2 He drank his coffee.   5 He had dinner in a restaurant.

3 He liked swimming in the river.   6 He wrote his diary at night.

Workbook page 81

3 Listen, read and say

1. cheap — expensive
2. clean — dirty
3. cold — hot
4. dark — light
   deep — shallow
5. hard — soft
6. heavy — light
7. long — short
8. new — old
9. old — young
10. short — tall
11. small — big

4 Say and point

Bill's coffee was too cold.

Workbook page 82

⑤ Read and match

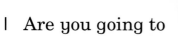

Are you going to wear those socks?

No, they're too dirty.

1 Are you going to wear those socks?

4 Are you going to use that ruler?

2 Are you going to ride that bike?

5 Are you going to buy those earrings?

6 Are you going to drink that tea?

3 Are you going to carry those books?

| a No, it's too cold. | b No, it's too short. | c No, it's too big. |
| d No, they're too expensive. | e No, they're too heavy. | f No, they're too dirty. |

⑥ Complete the sentences

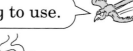

These pans are too dirty to use.

1 These pans ___

4 This tea ___

2 This necklace ___

5 These bags ___

3 These trousers ___

6 This bike ___

Workbook
page
83

7 Complete the postcard

Dear Kate,
I'm on holiday with 🐵. Yesterday we went 🐵🏊. In the afternoon we went for a 🏃. I carried 🐵 in my 🎒. I wanted to go to a 🪑 for dinner in the evening. But it was too expensive. So I cooked 🍳 on my stove.

Last night it rained. My 👕 got very wet. The ⛺ got wet too. I'm staying in a 🏢 now.

Tomorrow we're going to a 🏡 in the country. We're going to feed the 🐄🐄 and collect the 🥚🥚🥚. 🐵 is having a great time but I'm very tired! Love from Bill

8 Your work

Dear Susan,

I'm on holiday with mum and dad and my brother. We're staying in a hotel. The weather is very hot. It's too hot. It's too hot to play on the beach in the afternoon. We usually stay in our room and watch television. Yesterday we watched some cartoons. They were fantastic. Tomorrow we're going to the circus.

Love from
Alison

❶ Listen and read 😄

The princess and the pea

*O*nce upon a time there was a prince. The prince wanted a wife. He wanted to marry a princess. So the prince travelled around the world on his horse.

The prince met a lot of beautiful girls. 'I'm a princess,' the girls said. 'I'm from a royal family.'

But the prince didn't believe them. Some girls were too short to be princesses. Other girls were too tall.

Finally, the prince went back home. He went back to his palace. The prince was very sad. The king and queen were very sad too.

The next evening there was a terrible storm. The sky was black and it rained and rained. It was a terrible storm.

There was a knock at the palace door. A servant went to the door. He opened it. And he saw a beautiful girl outside in the rain.

The girl's clothes were wet. Her hair was wet. She was very cold. 'I'm a princess,' the girl said. 'Please can I come in?'

Workbook page
85

2 Listen, read and say 📼

1
prince

2
princess

3
king

4
queen

5
servants

3 Read and say

a   b

1   He travelled around the world.   d
2   She was very sad.
3   He opened the door.
4   He saw a beautiful girl.
5   She got wet in a storm.
6   She wanted to go into the palace.

c

d

e

4 Ask and answer

1   What did the prince want?   He wanted a wife.
2   How did he travel?
3   When did it rain?
4   Where did the servant go?

Workbook
page
86

78

5 **Listen and read** ⌨

The princess and the pea ░░░░░░░░░░░░░░░░░░░ PART 2

$\mathcal{T}$he servant took the girl to the queen. 'I'm a princess,' the girl said again. But the queen didn't believe her.

The queen and the servant went out of the room. 'A girl's staying with us tonight,' the queen said. 'Make a bed for her. Put twenty mattresses on the bed.'

The queen went into the kitchen. She picked up a pea. 'I'm going to put this pea under the mattresses,' she said. 'Princesses can't sleep when there's a pea under twenty mattresses.'

Then she went to the girl's bedroom. She put the pea under the mattresses. After that she went downstairs again. She spoke to the young girl. 'Your bed's ready,' she said. 'Sleep well.'

The next morning the queen went into the princess's bedroom. 'How did you sleep?' the queen asked. 'I slept badly,' the princess said. 'There was something in the bed. I don't know what it was. Perhaps it was a stone.'

The girl was a princess! The queen now believed her. Princesses can't sleep when there's a pea under twenty mattresses.

So the prince married the princess. But first he took the pea to the royal museum. And it's in the museum today!

6 **Put the pictures in order**   I picture d

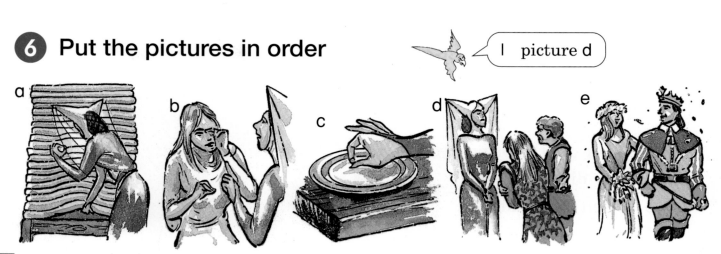

a   b   c   d   e

Workbook
page
87

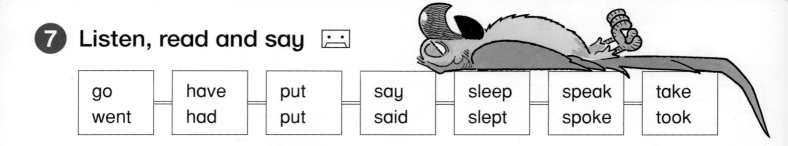

7 Listen, read and say 😀

go	have	put	say	sleep	speak	take
went	had	put	said	slept	spoke	took

8 Read and match

What did the girl say? — 'I'm a princess.'

1 What did the girl say?
2 Where did the queen go?
3 What did the queen do?
4 Where did the queen put the pea?
5 What did the queen say?
6 When did the queen go into the girl's bedroom?
7 How did the girl sleep?
8 What did the prince do?
9 Where did the prince take the pea?

a She went into the kitchen.
b 'Your bed is ready. Sleep well.'
c She slept badly.
d 'I'm a princess.'
e She picked up a pea.
f He took it to the royal museum.
g She went into her bedroom next morning.
h He married the princess.
i She put it under the mattresses.

9 Your game

1 The prince travelled around the world.

true

2 He travelled on foot.

false

Workbook page 88

1 Listen and say

2 True or false?

1 Adam is watching TV.  true
2 He wants to play dominoes.
3 He likes playing cards.
4 He wants to play chess.
5 He wants to go for a bike ride.

Workbook
page
91

3 Listen, read and say 😐

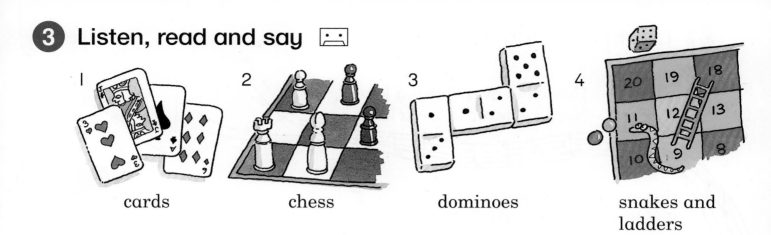

1 cards 2 chess 3 dominoes 4 snakes and ladders

4 Ask and answer about you

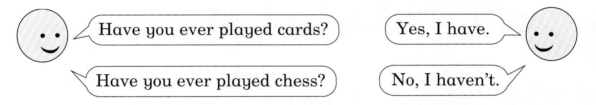

Have you ever played cards?   Yes, I have.

Have you ever played chess?   No, I haven't.

5 Listen, read and say 😐

mend	play	watch
mended	played	watched
mended	played	watched

drink	eat	fly	go	make
drank	ate	flew	went	made
drunk	eaten	flown	been	made

read	ride	see	write
read	rode	saw	wrote
read	ridden	seen	written

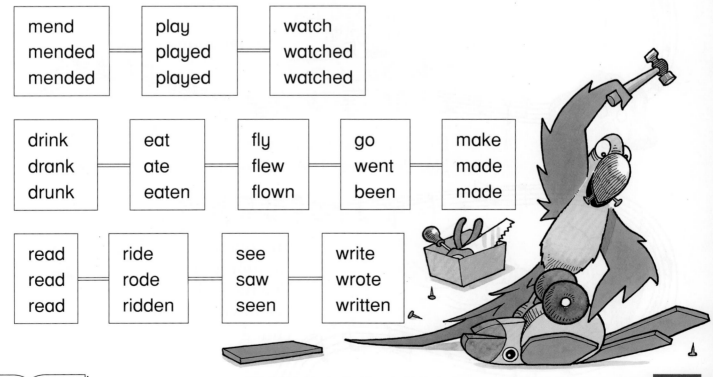

6 Listen and sing 😀

Have you ever flown a kite?
No, I've never flown a kite.

But as we get older,
We do more and more.
Look at me now!
I'm flying a kite.

So one day,
I can say,
'I have flown a kite.'

Have you ever made a cake?
No, I've never made a cake.

But as we get older,
We do more and more.
Look at me now!
I'm making a cake.

So one day,
I can say,
'I have made a cake.'

Have you ever been to Rome?
No, I've never been to Rome.

And one day,
I'm going to say,
'I've never been to Rome.
I've always lived at home.
That's where I'm going to stay.'

83

Workbook
page
93

7 Ask and answer about you

Have you ever been to a circus? **No, I haven't.**

1 Have you ever been to ___?

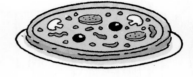

2 Have you ever eaten ___?

3 Have you ever read ___?

4 Have you ever ridden ___?

5 Have you ever seen ___?

6 Have you ever written ___?

8 Your game

I've been to a circus.

I've never been to a zoo.

I've never been to London.

I've been to the seaside.

1 Listen and say 😐

1 Have you got lots of videos?

Yes, I have. I like watching videos.

2 What's the most interesting film you've ever seen?

Aladdin.

3 Have you seen it?

Yes, I have. I didn't like it very much.

4 I've read the book too. I liked it.

5 What's the most interesting book you've ever read?

I don't know. I've read a lot of books.

6 OK, then. What's the most boring book you've ever read?

The most boring? Alice in Wonderland.

7 Alice in Wonderland! Oh, no!

What's the matter?

8 It's my favourite book!

2 Read and say

1 I liked Aladdin.
2 I didn't like Aladdin.
3 I liked Alice in Wonderland.
4 I didn't like Alice in Wonderland.

a

b

Workbook page 95

③ Ask and answer

1 Has Adam seen Aladdin?
2 Did he like it?

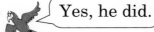

Yes, he has.

Yes, he did.

3 Has Sally seen Aladdin?
4 Did she like it?
5 Has Adam read Aladdin?

6 Did he like it?
7 Has Sally read Alice in Wonderland?
8 Did she like it?

④ Ask and answer

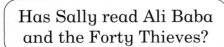

Has Sally read Ali Baba and the Forty Thieves?

No, she hasn't.

Has Adam read Ali Baba and the Forty Thieves?

Yes, he has.

Did he like it?

No, he didn't.

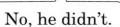

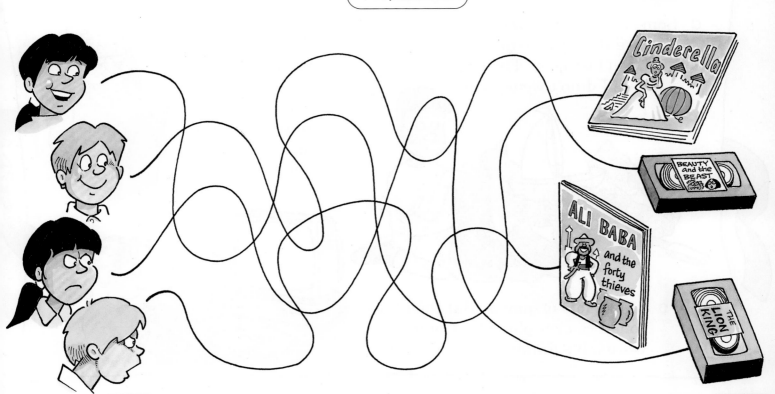

5 Listen and say

Adam's read Aladdin.
He's seen the film too.
He's read the book.
He's seen the film.
What about you?

Sally's seen The Lion King.
She's read the book too.
She's seen the film.
She's read the book.
What about you?

6 Read and match

1 What's the most interesting place you've ever visited?   (b)

2 What's the most boring present you've ever had?

3 What's the most interesting computer game you've ever played?

a Some socks. My grandmother gave them to me for my birthday last year. They were awful. I didn't wear them!

b I've travelled around the world many times. I've seen many interesting places. But the place I like best is my own home!

c I like lots of games. But the best one I've ever played is Computer Cards. It's fantastic. I play it a lot.

Workbook
page
97

7 Ask and answer about you

What's the most interesting place you've ever visited?

Paris is the most interesting place I've ever visited.

8 Listen and say

Have you been to London?
Have you been to Rome?
  Yes, I've been to London.
  Yes, I've been to Rome.
Did you like London?
Did you like Rome?
  Yes, I liked London.
  Yes, I liked Rome.
  But the best place I've been to . . . is my own home.

London

Rome

9 Your conversation

Have you ever played chess?

Did you like it?

What's the most interesting game you've ever played?

Yes, I have.

No, I didn't.

Snakes and ladders.

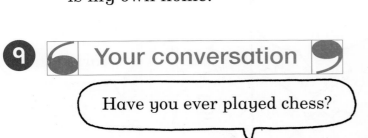

1 Listen and say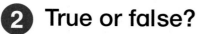

2 True or false?

1 Adam wants to go swimming.  true
2 He can't find his towel.
3 It's on his desk.
4 Adam's swimming shorts are red.
5 They're in the living room.
6 Adam can't see his goggles.

Workbook page 99

3 Listen and say

Have you seen my towel?
Yes, I have. I've seen it.
It's on your bed.

Have you seen my goggles?
Yes, I have. I've seen them.
They're on your head!

4 Listen, read and say

1 compass

2 penknife

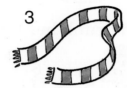
3 scarf

4 towel

5 glasses

6 goggles

7 shorts

8 trainers

5 Ask and answer

Have you seen Adam's compass?

Yes, I have. It's under the desk.

Have you seen his penknife?

No, I haven't.

Workbook
page
100

90

6 Ask, answer and point

1 Has Edward eaten his chips?

a No, he hasn't. He's eating them.

Yes, he has. b

2 Has Helen drunk her milk?

a

b

3 Has Adam read his story?

a

b

4 Has Sally written her letters?

a

b

5 Has Mum washed the dishes?

a

b

6 Has Dad watered the plants?

a

b

Workbook
page
101

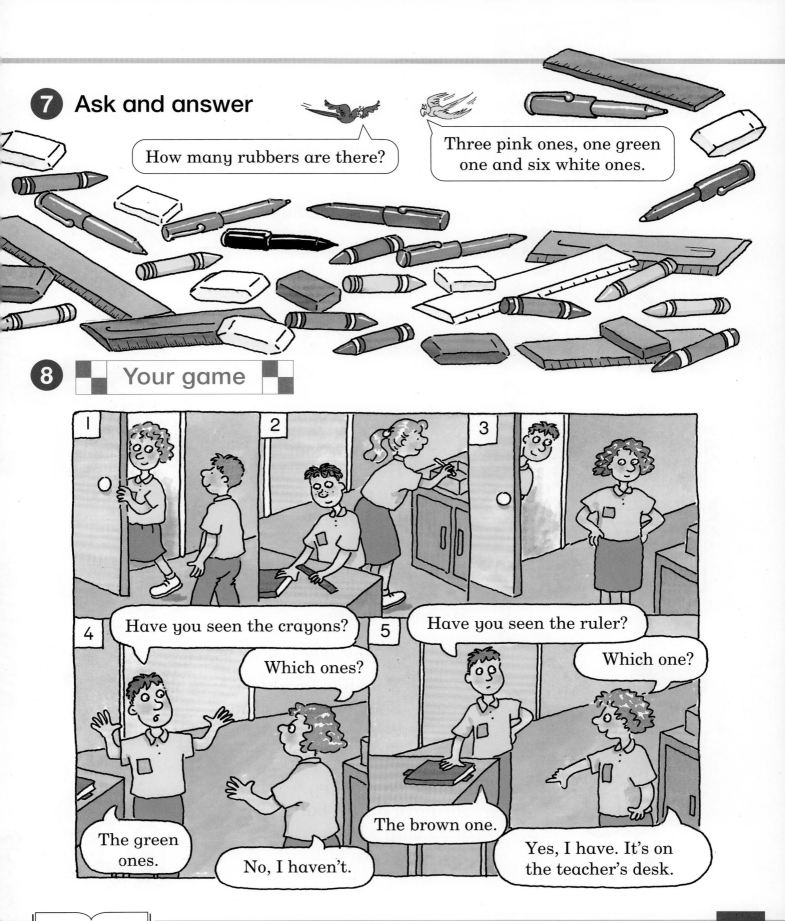

How many rubbers are there?

Three pink ones, one green one and six white ones.

8 Your game

1

2

3

4 Have you seen the crayons?

Which ones?

The green ones.

No, I haven't.

5 Have you seen the ruler?

Which one?

The brown one.

Yes, I have. It's on the teacher's desk.

UNIT 24

I Listen and sing

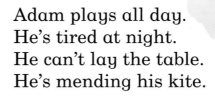

Adam plays all day.
He's tired at night.
He can't lay the table.
He's mending his kite.

Helen's Adam's sister.
She likes helping Dad.
She's often happy.
She's sometimes sad.

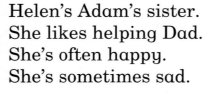

Old friends, old friends.
Old friends and new.
They all had fun.
What about you?

Edward went shopping.
He got a new toy.
He got a black hat.
He's a happy boy.

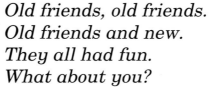

Bill works happily.
He works at the zoo.
He likes animals.
He's got a pet too.

Old friends, old friends ...

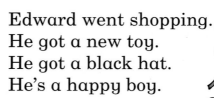

Kate had breakfast.
She put on her coat.
She went to London.
She went on a boat.

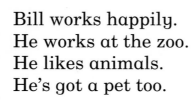

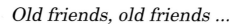

Minnie's a monkey.
She gave Kate a ball.
She's only a baby.
She's not very tall.

Old friends, old friends ...

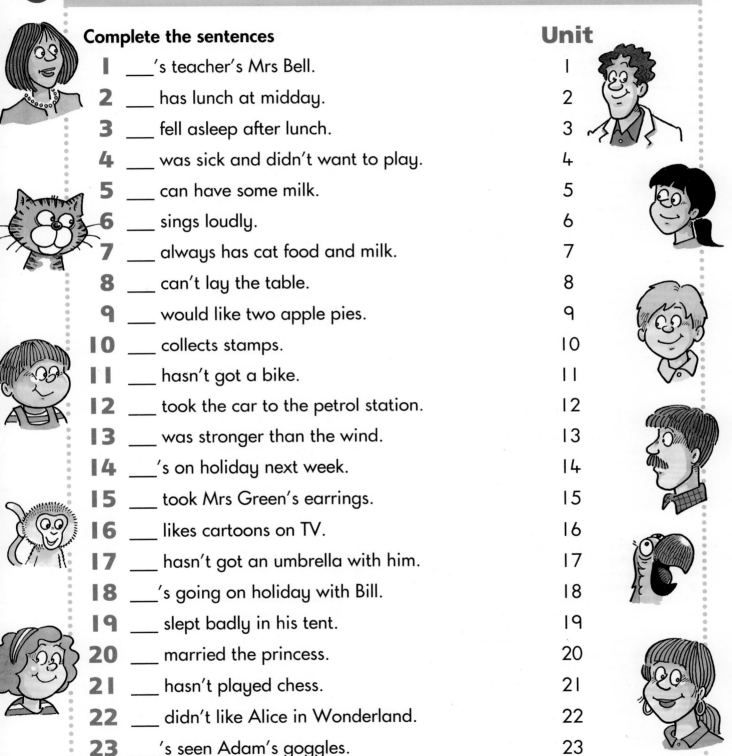

② YOUR QUIZ ??????????????

Complete the sentences   **Unit**

1   ___'s teacher's Mrs Bell.   1
2   ___ has lunch at midday.   2
3   ___ fell asleep after lunch.   3
4   ___ was sick and didn't want to play.   4
5   ___ can have some milk.   5
6   ___ sings loudly.   6
7   ___ always has cat food and milk.   7
8   ___ can't lay the table.   8
9   ___ would like two apple pies.   9
10 ___ collects stamps.   10
11 ___ hasn't got a bike.   11
12 ___ took the car to the petrol station.   12
13 ___ was stronger than the wind.   13
14 ___'s on holiday next week.   14
15 ___ took Mrs Green's earrings.   15
16 ___ likes cartoons on TV.   16
17 ___ hasn't got an umbrella with him.   17
18 ___'s going on holiday with Bill.   18
19 ___ slept badly in his tent.   19
20 ___ married the princess.   20
21 ___ hasn't played chess.   21
22 ___ didn't like Alice in Wonderland.   22
23 ___'s seen Adam's goggles.   23

SYLLABUS